JESUS
HIS ESSENTIAL
WISDOM

JESUS
HIS ESSENTIAL WISDOM

Edited by
CAROL KELLY-GANGI

FALL
RIVER
PRESS

To Mom and Dad with love and gratitude
for your living examples of faith.

The editor wishes to extend a special thanks to Reverend Abraham Lotha, M.A., Ph.D., and Reverend Michael Manning, M.D., S.T.L., for their helpful insights in the preparation of this book.

Scripture quotations are from *The New American Bible with Revised New Testament* © 1986, 1970 Confraternity of Christian Doctrine, Washington, D.C., and from *The New Jerusalem Bible,* Biblical text copyright © 1985 by Darton, Longman & Todd Ltd and Doubleday, a division of Random House, Inc. All rights reserved.

Book design by Lundquist Design, New York

Fall River Press
122 Fifth Avenue
New York, NY 10011

ISBN: 978-1-4351-2048-8

Printed and bound in the United States of America

10 9 8 7 6 5 4 3 2 1

Contents

Introduction

"**B**UT WHO DO YOU SAY THAT I AM?**"** Simon Peter said in reply, "You are the Messiah, the Son of the living God." Jesus said to him in reply, "Blessed are you, Simon son of Jonah. For flesh and blood has not revealed this to you, but my heavenly Father. And so I say to you, you are Peter, and upon this rock I will build my church, and the gates of the netherworld shall not prevail against it.

—*Matthew* 16:15–18

It has been said that no revolution has ever taken place that can be compared to that which resulted from the words of Jesus Christ. Indeed, millions of men and women through the ages have given their very lives to spread his teachings. In testament to the enduring impact Jesus has made on humanity, there are more than two billion Christians in the world today, which represents the greatest number of adherents for any of the world religions.

Jesus: His Essential Wisdom gathers together hundreds of quotations from and about Jesus and his teachings. The first and largest section of the book comprises the words of Jesus himself as drawn from the Gospels of Matthew, Mark, Luke, and John. In these selections, Jesus calls his followers to a new way of life focused on love, faith, repentance, charity, and humility. Arranged in thematic categories such as Love, Do Unto Others, Follow Me, Prayer and Faith, Sin and Forgiveness, and The Kingdom, the excerpts reflect the essence and spirit of the message that Jesus preached to his followers during the course of his public life. It is hoped that this arrangement of the words of Jesus—both revolutionary and profound—will help readers experience them in an altogether new way.

The second section of the book consists of quotations from what others have said about Jesus himself through the centuries. Saints and writers, religious leaders and world leaders, politicians and scientists, scholars and poets, each contribute their insights into what Jesus means to them and the unparalleled impact he has had on humankind. Thomas Merton and Pope Paul VI reflect on the nativity of Christ and what it meant for the world; Leo Tolstoy and Napoleon marvel at how Christ conquered the world not with armies, but with mildness, humility, and goodness. And Mahatma Gandhi proclaims that Christ belongs not just to Christianity but to the entire world.

The last section of the book consists of quotations from a diverse group of figures, both modern and historical, who offer their views of Jesus' teachings in particular and of the Christian faith in general. Charles Dickens extols the truth and beauty of Christianity; Desmond Tutu contemplates the role of suffering for Christians; and Mother Teresa challenges us to find Christ in the unlikeliest of places.

Whether you're a Christian on your own spiritual journey, or anyone interested in learning more about Jesus, his teachings, and his place in history, it is hoped that this collection will help in some small way to deepen your understanding of Jesus Christ.

—*Carol Kelly-Gangi*
Rumson, New Jersey, 2009

God the Father, the Son, and the Holy Spirit

Y OU SHALL LOVE THE LORD, your God, with all your heart, with all your soul, and with all your mind. This is the greatest and the first commandment. The second is like it: You shall love your neighbor as yourself. The whole law and the prophets depend on these two commandments.

—*Matthew* 22:37–40

It is written: 'One does not live by bread alone, but by every word that comes forth from the mouth of God.'

—*Matthew* 4:5

Therefore I tell you, do not worry about your life, what you
will eat [or drink], or about your body, what you will wear.
Is not life more than food and the body more than clothing?
Look at the birds in the sky; they do not sow or reap, they gather
nothing into barns, yet your heavenly Father feeds them. Are
not you more important than they? Can any of you by worrying
add a single moment to your life-span? Why are you anxious
about clothes? Learn from the way the wild flowers grow. They
do not work or spin. But I tell you that not even Solomon in
all his splendor was clothed like one of them. If God so clothes
the grass of the field, which grows today and is thrown into
the oven tomorrow, will he no much more provide for you,
O you of little faith? So do not worry and say, 'What are we
to eat?' or 'What are we to drink?' or 'What are we to wear?'
All these things the pagans seek. Your heavenly Father knows
that you need them all. But seek first the kingdom [of God] and
his righteousness, and all these things will be given you besides.
Do not worry about tomorrow; tomorrow will take care of
itself. Sufficient for a day is its own evil.

—*Matthew* 6:25–34

By human resources it is impossible, but not for God: because
for God everything is possible.

—*Mark* 10:27

For this is how God loved the world: he gave his only Son, so that everyone who believes in him may not perish but may have eternal life. For God sent his Son into the world not to judge the world, but so that through him the world might be saved.

—*John* 3:16–17

Why were you looking for me? Did you not know that I must be in my Father's house?

—*Luke* 2:49

It is for judgment that I have come into this world, so that those without sight may see and those with sight may become blind.

—*John* 9:39

To the other towns also I must proclaim the good news of the kingdom of God, because for this purpose I have been sent.

—*Luke* 4:43

In all truth I tell you, whoever listens to my words, and believes in the one who sent me, has eternal life; without being brought to judgment such a person has passed from death to life.

—*John* 5:24

✤

Anyone who has seen me has seen the Father, so how can you say, "Show us the Father"? Do you not believe that I am in the Father and the Father is in me? What I say to you I do not speak of my own accord: it is the Father, living in me, who is doing his works. You must believe me when I say that I am in the Father and the Father is in me; or at least believe it on the evidence of these works. In all truth I tell you, whoever believes in me will perform the same works as I do myself, and will perform even greater works, because I am going to the Father. Whatever you ask in my name I will do, so that the Father may be glorified in the Son.

—*John* 14:9–13

✤

The Son of Man must suffer greatly and be rejected by the elders, the chief priests, and the scribes, and be killed and on the third day be raised.

—*Luke* 9:22

What are you thinking in your hearts? Which is easier, to say, 'Your sins are forgiven,' or to say, 'Rise and walk'? But that you may know that the Son of Man has authority on earth to forgive sins . . . I say to you, rise, pick up your stretcher, and go home.

—*Luke* 5:22–24

Father, Upright One, the world has not known you, but I have known you, and these have known that you have sent me. I have made your name known to them and will continue to make it known, so that the love with which you loved me may be in them, and so that I may be in them.

—*John* 17:25–26

Go and tell John what you have seen and heard: the blind regain their sight, the lame walk, lepers are cleansed, the deaf hear, the dead are raised, the poor have the good news proclaimed to them. And blessed is the one who takes no offense at me.

—*Luke* 7:22–23

Father, if you are willing, take this cup away from me; still, not my will but yours be done.

 —Luke 22:42

Father, forgive them, they know not what they do.

 —Luke 23:34

Father, into your hands I commend my spirit.

 —Luke 23:46

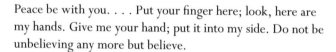

Peace be with you. . . . Put your finger here; look, here are my hands. Give me your hand; put it into my side. Do not be unbelieving any more but believe.

 —John 20:26–27

If you love me you will keep my commandments. I shall ask the Father, and he will give you another Paraclete to be with you for ever, the Spirit of truth whom the world can never accept since it neither sees nor knows him; but you know him, because he is with you, he is in you.

—*John* 14:15–17

❖

Everyone who speaks a word against the Son of Man will be forgiven, but the one who blasphemes against the holy Spirit will not be forgiven. When they take you before synagogues and before rulers and authorities, do not worry about how or what your defense will be or about what you are to say. For the holy Spirit will teach you at that moment what you should say.

—*Luke* 12:10–12

Love

LISTEN, ISRAEL, THE LORD OUR GOD is the one, only Lord, and you must love the Lord your God with all your heart, with all your soul, with all your mind and with all your strength. The second is this: You must love your neighbor as yourself. There is no commandment greater than these.

—*Mark* 12:29–31

I give you a new commandment: love one another; you must love one another just as I have loved you. It is by your love for one another, that everyone will recognize you as my disciples.

—*John* 13:34–35

You have heard that it was said, 'You shall love your neighbor and hate your enemy.' But I say to you, love your enemies, and pray for those who persecute you, that you may be children of your heavenly Father, for he makes his sun rise on the bad and the good, and causes rain to fall on the just and the unjust. For if you love those who love you, what recompense will you have? Do not the tax collectors do the same? And if you greet your brothers only, what is unusual about that? Do not the pagans do the same? So be perfect, just as your heavenly Father is perfect.

—*Matthew* 5:43–48

❖

You have heard that it was said, 'An eye for an eye and a tooth for a tooth,' But I say to you, offer no resistance to one who is evil. When someone strikes you on [your] right cheek, turn the other one to him as well. If anyone wants to go to law with you over your tunic, hand him your cloak as well. Should anyone press you into service for one mile, go with him for two miles. Give to the one who asks of you, and do not turn your back on one who wants to borrow.

—*Matthew* 5:38–42

I have loved you just as the Father has loved me. Remain in
my love. If you keep my commandments you will remain in
my love, just as I have kept my Father's commandments and
remain in his love.

—*John* 15:9–10

Whoever loves father or mother more than me is not worthy
of me, and whoever loves son or daughter more than me is
not worthy of me; and whoever does not take up his cross and
follow after me is not worthy of me. Whoever finds his life
will lose it, and whoever loses his life for my sake will find it.

—*Matthew* 10:37–39

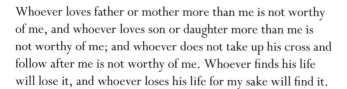

Anyone who loves me will keep my word, and my Father will
love him, and we shall come to him and make a home in him.
Anyone who does not love me does not keep my words. And
the word that you hear is not my own: it is the word of the
Father who sent me.

—*John* 14:23–24

Do Unto Others

Do to others whatever you would have them do to you. This is the law and the prophets.

—*Matthew* 7:12

❖

Do you understand what I have done to you? You call me Master and Lord, and rightly; so I am. If I, then, the Lord and Master, have washed your feet, you must wash each other's feet. I have given you an example so that you may copy what I have done to you.

—*John* 13:12–15

Therefore, if you bring your gift to the altar, and there recall that your brother has anything against you, leave your gift there at the altar, go first and be reconciled with your brother, and then come and offer your gift.

—*Matthew* 5:23–24

When you hold a lunch or a dinner, do not invite your friends or your brothers or your relatives or your wealthy neighbors, in case they may invite you back and you have repayment. Rather, when you hold a banquet, invite the poor, the crippled, the lame, the blind; blessed indeed will you be because of their inability to repay you. For you will be repaid at the resurrection of the righteous.

—*Luke* 14:12–14

But take care not to perform righteous deeds in order that people may see them; otherwise, you will have no recompense from your heavenly Father. When you give alms, do not blow a trumpet before you, as the hypocrites do in the synagogues and in the streets to win the praise of others. Amen, I say to you, they have received their reward. But when you give alms, do no let your left hand know what your right is doing, so that your almsgiving may be secret. And your Father who sees in secret will repay you.

—*Matthew* 6:1–4

Then they will answer and say, 'Lord, when did we see you hungry or thirsty or a stranger or naked or ill or in prison, and not minister to your needs?' He will answer them, 'Amen, I say to you, what you did not do for one of these least ones, you did not do for me.' And these will go off to eternal punishment, but the righteous to eternal life.

—*Matthew* 25:44–46

Stop judging and you will not be judged. Stop condemning and you will not be condemned. Forgive and you will be forgiven. Give and gifts will be given to you; a good measure, packed together, shaken down, and overflowing, will be poured into your lap. For the measure with which you measure will in return be measured out to you.

—*Luke* 6:37–38

A Call to Serve

TAKE NOTHING FOR THE JOURNEY, neither walking stick, nor sack, nor food, nor money, and let no one take a second tunic. Whatever house you enter, stay there and leave from there. And as for those who do not welcome you, when you leave that town, shake the dust from your feet in testimony against them.

—*Luke* 9:3–5

Come after me, and I will make you fishers of men.

—*Matthew* 4:20

You know that the rulers of the Gentiles lord it over them, and the great ones make their authority over them felt. But it shall not be so among you. Rather, whoever wishes to be great among you shall be your servant; whoever wishes to be first among you shall be your slave. Just so, the Son of Man did not come to be served but to serve and to give his life as a ransom for many.

—*Matthew* 20:25–28

❖

Blessed are the eyes that see what you see. For I say to you, many prophets and kings desired to see what you see, but did not see it, and to hear what you hear, but did not hear it.

—*Luke* 10:23–24

❖

Behold, I am sending you like sheep in the midst of wolves; so be shrewd as serpents and simple as doves. But beware of people, for they will hand you over to courts and scourge you in their synagogues, and you will be led before governors and kings for my sake as a witness before them and the pagans. When they hand you over, do not worry about how you are to speak or what you are to say. You will be given at that moment what you are to say. For it will not be you who speak but the Spirit of your Father speaking through you. Brother will hand over brother to death, and the father his child; children will rise up against parents and have them put to death. You will be hated by all because of my name, but whoever endures to the end will be saved.

—*Matthew* 10:16–22

Are not two sparrows sold for a small coin? Yet not one of them falls to the ground without your Father's knowledge. Even all the hairs of your head are counted. So do not be afraid; you are worth more than many sparrows. Everyone who acknowledges me before others I will acknowledge before my heavenly Father. But whoever denies me before others, I will deny before my heavenly Father.

—*Matthew* 10:30–33

Blessed are you, Simon son of Jonah. For flesh and blood has not revealed this to you, but my heavenly Father. And so I say to you, you are Peter, and upon this rock I will build my church, and the gates of the netherworld shall not prevail against it. I will give you the keys to the kingdom of heaven. Whatever you bind on earth shall be bound in heaven; and whatever you loose on earth shall be loosed in heaven.

—*Matthew* 16:17–19

This is my commandment: love one another, as I have loved
you. No one can have greater love than to lay down his life for
his friends. You are my friends, if you do what I command you.
I shall no longer call you servants, because a servant does not
know the master's business; I call you friends, because I have
made known to you everything I have learnt from my Father.
You did not choose me, no, I chose you; and I commissioned
you to go out and to bear fruit, fruit that will last; so that
the Father will give you anything you ask him in my name.
My command to you is to love one another.

—*John* 15:12–17

❖

Now you cannot follow me where I am going, but later you
shall follow me.

—*John* 13:36

❖

Simon, Simon, behold, behold Satan had demanded to sift all
of you like wheat, but I have prayed that your own faith may
not fail; and once you have turned back, you must strengthen
your brothers. . . . I tell you, Peter, before the cock crows this
day, you will deny three times that you know me.

—*Luke* 22:31–34

Simon, are you asleep? Had you not the strength to stay awake one hour? Stay awake and pray not to be put to the test. The spirit is willing enough, but human nature is weak.

—*Mark* 14:37–38

Why are you troubled? And why do questions arise in your hearts? Look at my hands and my feet, that it is I myself. Touch me and see, because a ghost does not have flesh and bones as you can see I have. . . . Thus it is written that the Messiah would suffer and rise from the dead on the third day and that repentance, for the forgiveness of sins, would be preached in his name to all the nations, beginning from Jerusalem. You are witnesses of these things. And [behold] I am sending the promise of my Father upon you; but stay in the city until you are clothed with power from on high.

—*Luke* 24:37–49

Peace be with you. As the Father sent me, so I am sending you. . . . Receive the Holy Spirit. If you forgive anyone's sins, they are forgiven; if you retain anyone's sins, they are retained.

—*John* 20:21–23

Go out to the whole world; proclaim the gospel to all creation. Whoever believes and is baptized will be saved; whoever does not believe will be condemned. These are the signs that will be associated with believers: in my name they will cast out devils; they will have the gift of tongues; they will pick up snakes in their hands and be unharmed should they drink deadly poison; they will lay their hands on the sick, who will recover.

—*Mark* 16:15–18

All power in heaven and on earth has been given to me. Go, therefore, and make disciples of all nations, baptizing them in the name of the Father, and of the Son, and of the holy Spirit, teaching them to observe all that I have commanded you. And behold, I am with you always, until the end of the age.

—*Matthew* 28: 18–20

Follow Me

Come to me, all you who labor and are burdened, and I will give you rest. Take my yoke upon you and learn from me, for I am meek and humble of heart; and you will find rest for yourselves. For my yoke is easy, and my burden light.

—*Matthew* 11:28–30

I am the light of the world; anyone who follows me will not be walking in the dark, but will have the light of life.

—*John* 8:12

I am the good shepherd; I know my own and my own know me, just as the Father knows me and I know the Father; and I lay down my life for my sheep. And there are other sheep I have that are not of this fold, and I must lead these too. They too will listen to my voice, and there will be only one flock, one shepherd. The Father loves me, because I lay down my life in order to take it up again. No one takes it from me; I lay it down of my own free will, and as I have power to lay it down, so I have power to take it up again, and this is the command I have received from my Father.

—*John* 10:14–18

I am the true vine, and my Father is the vinedresser. Every branch in me that bears no fruit he cuts away, and every branch that does bear fruit he prunes to make it bear even more. You are clean already, by means of the word that I have spoken to you Remain in me, as I in you. As a branch cannot bear fruit all by itself, unless it remains part of the vine, neither can you unless you remain in me. I am the vine, you are the branches. Whoever remains in me, with me in him, bears fruit in plenty; for cut off from me you can do nothing.

—*John* 15:1–5

I am the Way; I am Truth and Life. No one can come to the Father except through me. If you know me, you will know my Father too. From this moment you know him and have seen him.

—*John* 14:6–7

I am the bread of life. No one who comes to me will ever hunger; no one who believes in me will ever thirst.

—*John* 6:35

I am the resurrection. Anyone who believes in me, even though that person dies, will live, and whoever lives and believes in me will never die. Do you believe this?

—*John* 11:25–26

If anyone wants to be a follower of mine, let him renounce himself and take up his cross and follow me. Anyone who wants to save his life will lose it; but anyone who loses his life for my sake, and for the sake of the gospel, will save it. What gain, then, is it for anyone to win the whole world and forfeit his life? And indeed what can anyone offer in exchange for his life? For if anyone in this sinful and adulterous generation is ashamed of me and of my words, the Son of man will also be ashamed of him when he comes in the glory of his Father with the holy angels.

—*Mark* 8:34–38

It is not the healthy who need the doctor, but the sick. I came to call not the upright, but sinners.

—*Mark* 2:17

Who is my mother? Who are my brothers? . . . Here are my mother and my brothers. For whoever does the will of my heavenly Father is my brother, and sister, and mother.

—*Matthew* 12:48–50

Let the dead bury their dead. But you, go and proclaim the kingdom of God.

—*Luke* 9:60

Martha, Martha, you are anxious and worried about many things. There is need of only one thing. Mary has chosen the better part and it will not be taken from her.

—*Luke* 10:41–42

❖

In truth I tell you, there is no one who has left house, brothers, sisters, mother, father, children or land for my sake and for the sake of the gospel who will not receive a hundred times as much, houses, brothers, sisters, mothers, children and land—and persecutions too—now in this present time and, in the world to come, eternal life. Many who are first will be last, and the last, first.

—*Mark* 10:29–31

❖

Everyone who listens to these words of mine and acts on them will be like a wise man who built his house on rock. The rain fell, the floods came, and the winds blew and buffeted the house. But it did not collapse; it had been set solidly on rock. And everyone who listens to these words of mine but does not act on them will be like a fool who built his house on sand. The rain fell, the floods came, and the winds blew and buffeted the house. And it collapsed and was completely ruined.

—*Matthew* 7:24–27

Now the hour has come for the Son of man to be glorified. In all truth I tell you, unless a wheat grain falls into the earth and dies, it remains only a single grain; but if it dies it yields a rich harvest. Anyone who loves his life loses it; anyone who hates his life in this world will keep it for eternal life. Whoever serves me, must follow me, and my servant will be with me wherever I am. If anyone serves me, my Father will honor him.

—*John* 12:23–26

❖

Do not let your hearts be troubled. You trust in God, trust also in me. In my Father's house there are many places to live in; otherwise I would have told you. I am going now to prepare a place for you, and after I have gone and prepared you a place, I shall return to take you to myself, so that you may be with me where I am. You know the way to the place where I am going.

—*John* 14:1–4

❖

Sky and earth will pass away, but my words will not pass away.

—*Mark* 13:31

Prayer and Faith

THIS IS HOW YOU ARE TO PRAY:

Our Father in heaven,
hallowed be your name,
your kingdom come,
your will be done,
on earth as in heaven.
Give us today our daily bread;
and forgive us our debts,
as we forgive our debtors;
and do not subject us to the final test,
but deliver us from the evil one.

If you forgive others their transgressions, your heavenly Father
will forgive you. But if you do not forgive others, neither will
your Father forgive your transgressions.

—*Matthew* 6:9–15

Have faith in God. In truth I tell you, if anyone says to this mountain, "Be pulled up and thrown into the sea," with no doubt in his heart, but believing that what he says will happen, it will be done for him. I tell you, therefore, everything you ask and pray for, believe that you have it already, and it will be yours. And when you stand in prayer, forgive whatever you have against anybody, so that your Father in heaven may forgive your failings too.

Mark 11:22–25

✦

When you pray, do not be like the hypocrites, who love to stand and pray in the synagogues and on street corners so that others may see them. Amen, I say to you, they have received their reward. But when you pray, go to your inner room, close the door, and pray to your Father in secret. And your Father who sees in secret will repay you. In praying, do not babble like the pagans, who think that they will be heard because of their many words. Do not be like them. You Father knows what you need before you ask him.

—*Matthew* 6:5–8

Blessed are you who are poor,
>   for the kingdom of God is yours.
Blessed are you who are now hungry,
>   for you will be satisfied.
Blessed are you who are now weeping,
>   for you will laugh.
Blessed are you when people hate you,
>   and when they exclude and insult you,
>   and denounce your name as evil
>   on account of the Son of Man.

Rejoice and leap for joy on that day! Behold, your reward will be great in heaven. For their ancestors treated the prophets in the same way.

—*Luke* 6:20–23

❖

But woe to you who are rich,
>   for you have received your consolation.
But woe to you who are filled now,
>   for you will be hungry.
Woe to you who laugh now,
>   for you will grieve and weep.
Woe to you when all speak well of you,
>   for their ancestors treated the false prophets in this way.

—*Luke* 6:24–26

I give praise to you, Father, Lord of heaven and earth, for although you have hidden these things from the wise and the learned you have revealed them to the childlike. Yes, Father, such has been your gracious will. All things have been handed over to me by my Father. No one knows the Son except the Father, and no one knows the Father except the Son and anyone to whom the Son wishes to reveal him.

—*Matthew* 11:25–27

Ask and it will be given to you; seek and you will find; knock and the door will be opened to you. For everyone who asks, receives; and the one who seeks, finds; and to the one who knocks, the door will be opened. Which one of you would hand his son a stone when he asks for a loaf of bread, or a snake when he asks for a fish? If you then, who are wicked, know how to give good gifts to your children, how much more will your heavenly Father give good things to those who ask him.

—*Matthew* 7:7–11

Amen, I say to you, if you have faith and do not waver, not only will you do what has been done to the fig tree, but even if you say to this mountain, 'Be lifted up and thrown into the sea,' it will be done. Whatever you ask for in prayer with faith, you will receive.

—*Matthew* 21:21–22

If you have faith the size of a mustard seed, you would say to [this] mulberry tree, 'Be uprooted and planted in the sea,' and it would obey you.

—*Luke* 17:6

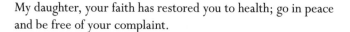

My daughter, your faith has restored you to health; go in peace and be free of your complaint.

—*Mark* 5:34

Unless you see signs and portents you will not believe!

—*John* 4:48

Ten were cleansed, were they not? Where are the other nine?
Has none but this foreigner returned to give thanks to God? . . .
Stand up and go; your faith has saved you.

—*Luke* 17:17–19

❖

You believe because you can see me. Blessed are those who
have not seen and yet believe.

—*John* 20:29

Sacraments

IN ALL TRUTH I TELL YOU, no one can enter the kingdom of God without being born through water and the Spirit; what is born of human nature is human; what is born of the Spirit is spirit. Do not be surprised when I say: You must be born from above. The wind blows where it pleases; you can hear its sound, but you cannot tell where it comes from or where it is going. So it is with everyone who is born of the Spirit.

—*John* 3:5–8

I am the living bread which has come down from heaven. Anyone who eats this bread will live for ever; and the bread that I shall give is my flesh, for the life of the world.

—*John* 6:51

In all truth I tell you, if you do not eat the flesh of the Son of man and drink his blood, you have no life in you. Anyone who does eat my flesh and drink my blood has eternal life; and I shall raise that person up on the last day. For my flesh is real food and my blood is real drink. Whoever eats my flesh and drinks my blood lives in me and I live in that person. As the living Father sent me and I draw life form the Father, so whoever eats me will also draw life from me. This is the bread which has come down from heaven; it is not like the bread our ancestors ate: they are dead, but anyone who eats this bread will live for ever.

—*John* 6:53–58

❖

Does this disturb you? What if you should see the Son of man ascend to where he was before? It is the spirit that gives life, the flesh has nothing to offer. The words I have spoken to you are spirit and they are life.

—*John* 6:61–63

Take this and share it among yourselves; for I tell you [that] from this time on I shall not drink of the fruit of the vine until the kingdom of God comes. . . . This is my body, which will be given for you; do this in memory of me. . . . This cup is the new covenant in my blood, which will be shed for you.

—*Luke* 22:17–20

Again, [amen,] I say to you, if two of you agree on earth about anything for which they are to pray, it shall be granted to them by my heavenly Father. For where two or three are gathered together in my name, there am I in the midst of them.

—*Matthew* 18:19–20

Sin and Forgiveness

I N ALL TRUTH I TELL YOU, everyone who commits sin is a slave.

—*John* 8:34

❖

Listen to me, all of you, and understand. Nothing that goes into someone from outside can make that person unclean; it is the things that come out of someone that make that person unclean. Anyone who has ears for listening should listen! . . . For it is from within, from the heart, that evil intentions emerge: fornication, theft, murder, adultery, avarice, malice, deceit, indecency, envy, slander, pride, folly. All these evil things come from within and make a person unclean.

—*Mark* 7:14–23

If your right eye causes you to sin, tear it out and throw it away. It is better for you to lose one of your members than to have your whole body thrown into Gehenna. And if your right hand causes you to sin, cut it off and throw it away. It is better for you to lose one of your members than to have your whole body go into Gehenna.

—*Matthew* 5:29–30

Things that cause sin will inevitably occur, but woe to the person through whom they occur. It would be better for him if a millstone were put around his neck and he be thrown into the sea than for him to cause one of these little ones to sin. Be on your guard! If your bother sins, rebuke him; and if he repents, forgive him. And if he wrongs you seven times saying, 'I am sorry,' you should forgive him.

—*Luke* 17:1–4

I tell you, on the day of judgment people will render an account for every careless word they speak. By your words you will be acquitted, and by your words you will be condemned.

—*Matthew* 12:36–37

Stop judging, that you may not be judged. For as you judge, so will you be judged, and the measure with which you measure will be measured out to you. Why do you notice the splinter in your brother's eye, but do not perceive the wooden beam in your own eye? How can you say to your brother, 'Let me remove that splinter from your eye,' while the wooden beam is in your eye? You hypocrite, remove the wooden beam from your eye first; then you will see clearly to remove the splinter from your brother's eye.

—*Matthew* 7:1–5

❖

Let the one among you who is guiltless be the first to throw a stone at her.

—*John* 8:7

❖

Beware of the scribes who like to walk about in long robes, to be greeted respectfully in the market squares, to take the front seats in the synagogues and the places of honor at banquets; these are the men who devour the property of widows and for show offer long prayers. The more severe will be the sentence they receive.

—*Mark* 12:38–40

Woe to you Pharisees! You pay tithes of mint and of rue and of every garden herb, but you pay no attention to judgment and to love for God. These you should have done, without overlooking the others. Woe to you Pharisees! You love the seat of honor in synagogues and greetings in marketplaces. Woe to you! You are like unseen graves over which people unknowingly walk.

—*Luke* 11:42–44

❖

Do you see this woman? When I entered your house, you did not give me water for my feet, but she has bathed them with her tears and wiped them with her hair. You did not give me a kiss, but she has not ceased kissing my feet since the time I entered. You did not anoint my head with oil, but she anointed my feet with ointment. So I tell you, her many sins have been forgiven; hence, she has shown great love. But the one to whom little is forgiven, loves little. . . . Your faith has saved you; go in peace.

—*Luke* 7:44–50

Whoever is not with me is against me, and whoever does not gather with me scatters. Therefore, I say to you, every sin and blasphemy will be forgiven people, but blasphemy against the Spirit will not be forgiven. And whoever speaks a word against the Son of Man will be forgiven; but whoever speaks against the holy Spirit will not be forgiven, either in this age or in the age to come.

—*Matthew* 12:30–32

✦

What man among you having a hundred sheep and losing one of them would not leave the ninety-nine in the desert and go after the lost one until he finds it? And when he does find it, he sets it on his shoulders with great joy and, upon his arrival home, he calls together his friends and neighbors and says to them, 'Rejoice with me because I have found my lost sheep.' I tell you, in just the same way there will be more joy in heaven over one sinner who repents than over ninety-nine righteous people who have no need of repentance.

—*Luke* 15:4–7

Or what woman having ten coins and losing one would not light a lamp and sweep the house, searching carefully until she finds it? And when she does find it, she calls together her friends and neighbors and says to them, 'Rejoice with me because I have found the coin that I lost.' In just the same way, I tell you, there will be rejoicing among the angels of God over one sinner who repents.

—*Luke* 15:8–10

The Material World

NO ONE CAN SERVE TWO MASTERS. He will either hate one and love the other, or be devoted to one and despise the other. You cannot serve God and mammon.

—*Matthew* 6:24

✤

Take care to guard against all greed, for though one may be rich, one's life does not consist of possessions.

—*Luke* 12:15

Pay Caesar what belongs to Caesar—and God what belongs to God.

—*Mark* 12:17

❖

How hard it is for those who have wealth to enter the kingdom of God! For it is easier for a camel to pass through the eye of a needle than for a rich person to enter the kingdom of God.

—*Luke* 18:24–25

❖

In truth I tell you, this poor widow has put more in than all who have contributed to the treasury; for they have all put in money they could spare, but she in her poverty has put in everything she possessed, all she had to life on.

—*Mark* 12:43–44

Do not store up for yourselves treasures on earth, where moth and decay destroy, and thieves break in and steal. But store up treasures in heaven, where neither moth nor decay destroy, nor thieves break in and steal. For where your treasure is, there also will your heart be.

—*Matthew* 6:19–21

❖

If you wish to be perfect, go, sell what you have and give to [the] poor, and you will have treasure in heaven. Then come, follow me.

—*Matthew* 19:21

The Law

Do not think that I have come to abolish the law or the prophets. I have come not to abolish but to fulfill. Amen, I say to you, until heaven and earth pass away, not the smallest letter or the smallest part of a letter will pass from the law, until all things have taken place. Therefore, whoever breaks one of the least of these commandments and teaches others to do so will be called least in the kingdom of heaven. But whoever obeys and teaches these commandments will be called greatest in the kingdom of heaven. I tell you, unless your righteousness surpasses that of the scribes and Pharisees, you will not enter into the kingdom of heaven.

—*Matthew 5:17–20*

The Sabbath was made for man, not man for the Sabbath; so the Son of man is master even of the Sabbath.

—*Mark* 2:27–28

✤

I ask you, is it lawful to do good on the Sabbath rather than to do evil, to save life rather than to destroy it?

—*Luke* 6:9

✤

Which one of you who has a sheep that falls into a pit on the Sabbath will not take hold of it and lift it out? How much more valuable a person is than a sheep. So it is lawful to do good on the Sabbath.

—*Matthew* 12:11–12

Woe also to you scholars of the law! You impose on people burdens hard to carry, but you yourselves do not lift one finger to touch them. Woe to you! You build the memorials of the prophets whom your ancestors killed. Consequently, you bear witness and give consent to the deeds of your ancestors, for they killed them and you do the building. . . . Woe to you, scholars of the law! You have taken away the key of knowledge. You yourselves did not enter and you stopped those trying to enter.

—*Luke* 11:46–48, 52

The Kingdom

THE COMING OF THE KINGDOM OF GOD cannot be observed, and no one will announce, 'Look, here it is,' or, 'There it is,' For behold, the kingdom of God is among you.

—*Luke* 17:20–21

❖

What can we say that the kingdom is like? What parable can we find for it? It is like a mustard seed which, at the time of its sowing, is the smallest of all the seeds on earth. Yet once it is sown it grows into the biggest shrub of them all and puts out big branches so that the birds of the air can shelter in its shade.

—*Mark* 4:30–32

The kingdom of heaven is like yeast that a woman took and mixed with three measures of wheat flour until the whole batch was leavened.

—*Matthew* 13:33

The kingdom of heaven is like a treasure buried in a field, which a person finds and hides again, and out of joy goes and sells all that he has and buys that field.

—*Matthew* 13:44

Again, the kingdom of heaven is like a net thrown into the sea, which collects fish of every kind. When it is full they haul it ashore and sit down to put what is good into buckets. What is bad they throw away. Thus it will be at the end of the age. The angels will go out and separate the wicked from the righteous and throw them into the fiery furnace, where there will be wailing and grinding of teeth.

—*Matthew* 13:47–50

Let the little children come to me; do not stop them; for it is to such as these that the kingdom of God belongs. In truth I tell you, anyone who does not welcome the kingdom of God like a little child will never enter it.

—*Mark* 10:14–15

Thus, the last will be first, and the first will be last.

—*Matthew* 20: 16

Not everyone who says to me, 'Lord, Lord,' will enter the kingdom of heaven, but only the one who does the will of my Father in heaven. Many will say to me on that day, 'Lord, Lord, did we not prophesy in your name? Did we not drive out demons in your name? Did we not do might deeds in your name?' Then I will declare to them solemnly, 'I never knew you. Depart from me, you evildoers.'

—*Matthew* 7:21–23

Mine is not a kingdom of this world; if my kingdom were of this world, my men would have fought to prevent my being surrendered to the Jews. As it is, my kingdom does not belong here.

—John 18:36

Beware that your hearts do not become drowsy from carousing and drunkenness and the anxieties of daily life, and that day catch you by surprise like a trap. For that day will assault everyone who lives on the face of the earth. Be vigilant at all times and pray that you have the strength to escape the tribulations that are imminent and to stand before the Son of Man.

—Luke 21:34–36

But as for that day or hour, nobody knows it, neither the angels in heaven, nor the Son; no one but the Father. Be on your guard, stay awake, because you never know when the time will come.

—Mark 13:32–33

Do not be afraid any longer, little flock, for your Father is pleased to give you the kingdom. Sell your belongings and give alms. Provide money bags for yourselves that do not wear out, an inexhaustible treasure in heaven that no thief can reach nor moth destroy. For where your treasure is, there also will your heart be.

—*Luke* 12:32–34

Words of Wisdom

THE LAMP OF THE BODY IS THE EYE. If your eye is sound, your whole body will be filled with light; but if your eye is bad, your whole body will be in darkness. And if the light in you is darkness, how great will the darkness be.

—*Matthew 6:22–23*

❖

Why do you notice the splinter in your brother's eye, but do not perceive the wooden beam in your own eye?

—*Matthew 7:3*

Beware of false prophets, who come to you in sheep's clothing, but underneath are ravenous wolves. By their fruits you will know them. Do people pick grapes from thornbushes, or figs from thistles? Just so, every good tree bears good fruit, and a rotten tree bears bad fruit. A good tree cannot bear bad fruit, nor can a rotten tree bear good fruit. Every tree that does not bear good fruit will be cut down and thrown into the fire. So by their fruits you will know them.

—Matthew 7:15–20

❖

A good person out of the store of goodness in his heart produces good, but an evil person out of a store of evil produces evil; for from the fullness of the heart the mouth speaks.

—Luke 6:45

❖

If a blind person leads a blind person, both will fall into a pit.

—Matthew 15:14

Do not give what is holy to dogs, or throw your pearls before swine, lest they trample them underfoot, and turn and tear you to pieces.

—*Matthew* 7:6

❖

Put your sword back into its sheath, for all who take the sword will perish by the sword.

—*Matthew* 26:52

❖

You are the salt of the earth. But if salt loses its taste, with what can it be seasoned? It is no longer good for anything but to be thrown out and trampled underfoot. You are the light of the world. A city set on a mountain cannot be hidden. Nor do they light a lamp and then put it under a bushel basket; it is set on a lampstand, where it gives light to all in the house. Just so, your light must shine before others, that they may see your good deeds and glorify your heavenly Father.

—*Matthew* 5: 13–16

What Others Have Said About Jesus

NOW THERE WERE SHEPHERDS IN THAT REGION living in the fields and keeping the night watch over their flock. The angel of the Lord appeared to them and the glory of the Lord shone around them, and they were struck with great fear. The angel said to them, "Do not be afraid; for behold, I proclaim to you good news of great joy that will be for all the people. For today in the city of David a savior has been born for you who is Messiah and Lord. And this will be a sign for you: you will find an infant wrapped in swaddling clothes and lying in a manger." And suddenly there was a multitude of the heavenly host with the angel, praising God and saying:

"Glory to God in the highest
and on earth peace to those on whom
his favor rests."

—*Luke 2:8–14*

We consider Christmas as the encounter, the great encounter, the historical encounter, the decisive encounter, between God and mankind. He who has faith knows this truly; let him rejoice.

—*Pope Paul VI* (1897–1978)

In the Nativity of Christ, the Great Joy is announced, in which all the ambiguities are swept aside and all men are confronted with the clear possibility of a decision that will not only help them to put together the pieces of lives wrecked in individual failure but will even make sense out of the lives of all men of all time.

—*Thomas Merton* (1915–1968)

Jesus is God-with-us, Emmanuel. The great mystery of God becoming human is God's desire to be loved by us. By becoming a vulnerable child, completely dependent on human care, God wants to take away all distance between the human and the divine.

—*Henri J. M. Nouwen, Dutch-born Catholic priest and writer* (1932–1996)

The birth of Jesus is the sunrise of the Bible. Towards this point the aspirations of the prophets and the poems of the psalmists were directed as the heads of flowers are turned toward the dawn. From this point a new day began to flow very silently over the world—a day of faith and freedom, a day of hope and love. When we remember the high meaning that has come into human life and the clear light that has flooded softly down from the manger-cradle in Bethlehem of Judea, we do not wonder that mankind has learned to reckon history from the birthday of Jesus, and to date all events by the years before or after the Nativity of Christ.

—*Henry Van Dyke, American clergyman and writer*
(1852–1933)

❖

He is mediator because He is both God and man. He holds within Himself the entire intimate world of divinity, the entire Mystery of the Trinity, and the mystery both of temporal life and of immortality. He is true man. In Him the divine is not confused with the human. There remains something essentially divine. But at the same time Christ is so human! Thanks to this, the entire world of men, the entire history of humanity, finds in Him its expression before God.

—*Pope John Paul II (1920–2005)*

Maker of the sun,
He is made under the sun.
In the Father he remains,
From his mother he goes forth.
Creator of heaven and earth,
He was born on earth under heaven.
Unspeakably wise,
He is wisely speechless.
Filling the world,
He lies in a manger.
Ruler of the stars,
He nurses at his mother's bosom.
He is both great in the nature of God,
and small in the form of a servant.

—*St. Augustine* (354–430)

Jesus Christ, the condescension of divinity, and the exaltation of humanity.

—*Phillips Brooks, American clergyman* (1835–1893)

Christ is God clothed with human nature.

—*Benjamin Whichcote, English theologian* (1609–1683)

Through Christ we see as in a mirror the spotless and excellent face of God.

—*St. Clement of Rome* (d. c. 99)

Christ was not half a God and half a man; he was perfectly God and perfectly man.

—*James Stalker, Scottish clergyman and writer* (1848–1927)

The properties of each nature and substance were preserved in their totality, and came together to form one person. Humility was assumed by majesty, weakness by strength, mortality by eternity; and to pay the debt that we had incurred, an inviolable nature was united to a nature that can suffer.

—*St. Leo the Great* (d. 461)

He does not cease to be God because He becomes Man,
nor fail to be Man because He remains forever God. This is
the true faith for human blessedness, to preach at once the
Godhead and the manhood, to confess the Word and the flesh,
neither forgetting the God, because He is man, nor ignoring
the flesh, because He is the Word.

—*St. Hilary of Poitiers* (c. 315–367)

If God never became flesh, like us, he could neither redeem
us nor reveal to us his promise of eternal life. It is only by
becoming like us that God can make us like him, restoring us
to his image.

—*St. Irenaeus* (c. 130–c.208)

When you wonder about the mystery of yourself, look to
Christ, who gives you the meaning of life. When you wonder
what it means to be a mature person, look to Christ, who is
the fulfillness of humanity. And when you wonder about your
role in the future of the world look to Christ.

—*Pope John Paul II*

After Jesus was baptized, he came up from the water and behold, the heavens were opened [for him], and he saw the Spirit of God descending like a dove [and] coming upon him. And a voice came from the heavens, saying, "This is my beloved Son, with whom I am well pleased."

—*Matthew* 3:16–17

How sweet the name of Jesus sounds
    In a believer's ear!
It soothes his sorrows, heals his wounds,
    And drives away his fear.

—*John Newton, English clergyman* (1725–1807)

When we speak about wisdom, we are speaking of Christ. When we speak about virtue, we are speaking of Christ. When we speak about justice, we are speaking of Christ. When we speak about peace, we are speaking of Christ. When we speak about truth and life and redemption, we are speaking of Christ.

—*St. Ambrose of Milan* (340–397)

I believe there is nothing lovelier, deeper, more sympathetic and more perfect than the Saviour; I say to myself with jealous love that not only is there on one else like Him, but that there could be no one. I would say even more. If any one could prove to me that Christ is outside the truth, and if the truth really did exclude Christ, I should prefer to stay with Christ and not with truth. There is in the world only one figure of absolute beauty: Christ. That infinitely lovely figure is as a matter of course an infinite marvel.

—*Fyodor Dostoyevsky* (1821–1888), *from* The Brothers Karamazov

I have read in Plato and Cicero sayings that are very wise and very beautiful; but I never read in either of them: "Come unto me all ye that labour and are heavy laden."

—*St. Augustine*

I am amazed by the sayings of Christ. They seem truer than anything I have ever read. And they certainly turn the world upside down.

—*Katharine Butler Hathaway, American writer* (1890–1942)

Christ appeared not as a philosopher or wordy doctor, or noisy disputer, or even as a wise and learned scribe, but he talked with people in complete simplicity, showing them the way of the truth in the way he lived, his goodness and his miracles.

—*Blessed Angela of Foligno, Italian mystic* (1248–1309)

Jesus was to be invited by men and women many more times during the course of his teaching activity. He would accept their invitations. He would relate to them, sit down at table and talk.

—*Pope John Paul II*

No revolution that has ever taken place in society can be compared to that which has been produced by the words of Jesus Christ.

—*Mark Hopkins, American educator and theologian* (1802–1887)

Jesus needs neither books nor Doctors of Divinity in order to instruct souls; He, the Doctor of Doctors, He teaches without noise of words.

—*St. Thérèse of Lisieux* (1873–1897)

The teaching of Jesus astonished and delighted all the people, because it promised liberty to all. The teaching of Jesus was the fulfillment of the prophesies of Isaiah, that the chosen of God should bring light unto men, should defeat evil, and should establish truth, not by violence, but by mildness, humility, and goodness.

—*Leo Tolstoy* (1828–1910)

Meekness was the method that Jesus used with the apostles. He put up with their ignorance and roughness and even their infidelity. He treated sinners with a kindness and affection that caused some to be shocked, others to be scandalized, and still others to gain hope in God's mercy. Thus, he bade us to be gentle and humble of heart.

—*St. John Bosco* (1815–1888)

Gentle Jesus, meek and mild, Look upon a little child; Pity my simplicity, Suffer me to come to thee.

—*Charles Wesley, English religious leader* (1707–1788)

Jesus, the Blessed One, is gentle. Even though he speaks with great fervor and biting criticism against all forms of hypocrisy and is not afraid to attack deception, vanity, manipulation, and oppression, his heart is a gentle heart. He won't break the crushed reed or snuff the faltering wick.

—*Henri J. M. Nouwen*

When Jesus took bread, blessed it, broke it, and give it to his disciples, he summarized in these gestures his own life. Jesus is chosen from all eternity, blessed at his baptism in the Jordan River, broken on the cross, and given as bread to the world. Being chosen, blessed, broken, and given is the sacred journey of the Son of God, Jesus the Christ.

—*Henri J. M. Nouwen*

Those holy fields
Over whose acres walk'd those blessed feet
Which, fourteen hundred years ago, were nail'd
For our advantage on the bitter cross.

—*William Shakespeare* (1564–1616)

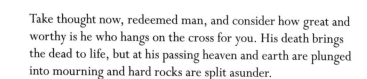

Take thought now, redeemed man, and consider how great and worthy is he who hangs on the cross for you. His death brings the dead to life, but at his passing heaven and earth are plunged into mourning and hard rocks are split asunder.

—*St. Bonaventure* (1221–1274)

A man who was completely innocent, offered himself as a sacrifice for the good of others, including his enemies, and became the ransom of the world. It was a perfect act.

—*Mahatma Gandhi* (1869–1948)

The High Priest asked him, "and he said unto him, Art though the Christ, the Son of the Blessed?" And Jesus said, "I am." And when he said that, he set in motion his trial and death. According to Mark, this is the only time he actually said it. And saying it, he set up his death. He knew what he was doing.

> And he did it.
> And he chose to do it.
> Of his own will.

—*Lois A. Cheney, American professor and writer* (b. 1931)

❖

I shall remind myself of the labors He undertook in preaching, of his weariness while traveling, of the temptations He suffered while fasting, of his vigils while praying, and of the tears He shed out of compassion. I will remember, moreover, his sorrows, and the insults, spittle, blows, ridicule, rebukes, nails, and all the rest that rained down upon Him in abundance.

—*St. Bernard of Clairvaux* (1090–1153)

Christ is arisen,
 Joy to thee, mortal!
Out of His prison,
 Forth from its portal!
Christ is not sleeping,
 Seek Him no longer;
Strong was His keeping,
 Jesus was stronger.

Christ is arisen,
 Seek Him not here;
Lonely His prison,
 Empty His bier;
Vain His entombing,
 Spices and lawn,

Vain the perfuming,
 Jesus is gone.

Christ is arisen,
 Joy to thee, mortal!
Empty His prison,
 Broken its portal

Rising, He giveth
 His shroud to the sod;
Risen, He liveth,
And liveth to God.

—*Johann Wolfgang von Goethe* (1749–1832)

I know men and I tell you that Jesus Christ is no mere man. Between Him and every other person in the world there is no possible term of comparison. Alexander, Caesar, Charlemagne, and I have founded empires. But on what did we rest the creation of our genius? Upon force. Jesus Christ founded His empire upon love; and at this hour millions of men would die for Him.

—*Napoleon Bonaparte* (1769–1821)

✤

Out of love the Lord took us to himself; because he loved us and it was God's will, our Lord Jesus Christ gave his life's blood for us—he gave his body for our body, his soul for our soul.

—*St. Clement of Rome*

✤

Love is what endowed Christ's suffering and death with its infinite value and power. Opponents of Christianity sometimes claim that other people have suffered more than Jesus. Yet no one has ever loved more. And nowhere is Jesus' love more active than in His obedience unto death.

—*Scott Hahn, American professor, theologian, and writer* (b. 1957)

Jesus loves me—this I know. For the Bible tells me so.

—*Susan Warner, American evangelical writer* (1819–1885)

No man ever loved like Jesus. He taught the blind to see and the dumb to speak. He died on the cross to save us. He bore our sins. And now God says, "Because He did, I can forgive you."

—*Billy Graham* (b. 1918)

Jesus Christ was an extremist for love, truth, and goodness.

—*Martin Luther King, Jr.* (1929–1968)

To Jesus religion was *service*. It was love of God *and* love of men. Ritual was irrelevant compared with love in action. To Jesus the most important thing in the world was not the correct performance of a ritual, but the spontaneous answer to the cry of human need.

—*William Barclay, Scottish theologian and writer* (1907–1978)

And when people speak ill of the poor and miserable, think how Jesus Christ went among them, and taught them, and thought them worthy of His care. And always pity them yourselves, and think as ell of them as you can.

—*Charles Dickens* (1812–1870)

Christ cannot be separated from the miraculous; His birth, His ministrations and His resurrection, all involve the miraculous, and the change which His religion works in the human heart is a continuing miracle.

—*William Jennings Bryan, American politician* (1860–1925)

Jesus came to meet men and women, to heal the sick and the suffering, to free those possessed by devils and to raise the dead. He gave himself on the cross and rose again from the dead, revealing that he is the Lord of life—the author and the source of life without end.

—*Pope John Paul II*

Our true friend. Whom alone we can trust, is Jesus Christ. When I depend upon Him, I feel so strong that I think I could stand firm against the whole world.

—*St. Teresa of Avila* (1515–1582)

✥

The most potent figure, not only in the history of religion, but in world history as a whole, is Jesus Christ: the maker of one of the few revolutions which have lasted. Millions of men and women for century after century have found his life and teaching overwhelmingly significant and moving. And there is ample reason . . . why this should still be so.

—*Michael Grant, English classical historian and writer* (1914–2004)

✥

Jesus Christ is to me the outstanding personality of all time, all history, both as Son of God and as Son of Man. Everything he ever said or did has value for us today and that is something you can say of no other man, dead or alive. There is no easy middle ground to stroll upon. You either accept Jesus or reject him.

—*Sholem Asch, Polish nationalist and playwright* (1880–1957)

Jesus of Nazareth, without money and arms, conquered more millions than Alexander the Great, Caesar, Mohammed, and Napoleon; without science and learning, he shed more light on things human and divine than all philosophers and scholars combined; without the eloquence of school, he spoke such words of life as were never spoken before or since, and produced effects which lie beyond the reach of orator or poet; without writing a single line, he set more pens in motion, and furnished themes for more sermons, orations, discussions, learned volumes, works of art, and songs of praise than the whole army of great men of ancient and modern times.

—*Phillip Schaff, American theologian* (1819–1893)

The unique impression of Jesus upon mankind—whose name is not so much written as ploughed into the history of the world—is proof of the subtle virtue of this infusion. Jesus belonged to the race of prophets. He saw with open eyes the mystery of the soul. One man was true to what is in you and me. He, as I think, is the only soul in history who has appreciated the worth of man.

—*Ralph Waldo Emerson* (1803–1882)

I am an historian, I am not a believer, but I must confess as a historian that this penniless preacher from Nazareth is irrevocably the very center of history. Jesus Christ is easily the most dominant figure in all history.

—*H. G. Wells* (1866–1946)

✤

More books have been written, more songs have been composed, and more lives have been given in the name of Jesus Christ than of any other person who ever lived. The beginning of his life on earth was the beginning of our calendar, and the end of his life on earth was the most dramatic event in history. Even though Jesus left this world nearly two thousand years ago, more than two billion people living today identify with him in one way or another by calling themselves Christians. By all measurements, Jesus is the central figure of the human race.

—*Bruce Bickel and Stan Jantz, American inspirational speakers and writers*

Christ is the most unique person in history. No man can write a history of the human race without giving first and foremost place to the penniless teacher of Nazareth.

—*H. G. Wells*

As a child I received instruction both in the Bible and in the Talmud. I am a Jew, but I am enthralled by the luminous figure of the Nazarene. . . . No one can read the Gospels without feeling the actual presence of Jesus. His personality pulsates in every word. No myth is filled with such life.

—*Albert Einstein (1879–1955)*

Jesus picked up twelve men from the bottom ranks of business and forged them into an organization that conquered the world.

—*Bruce Barton, American advertising executive (1886–1967)*

Jesus is not a blue-eyed right-winger, as some have implied; nor is he a guilt-ridden liberal or compromising centrist. Jesus is the one who entered the world among the dispossessed and the outcasts to announce an entirely new way of thinking and living. The way of Jesus and the prophets isn't just a welfare program; it calls for a change of heart, a revolution of the spirit, a transformation of our consciousness.

—*Jim Wallis, American evangelical writer and political activist* (b. 1948)

Jesus means something to our world because a mighty spiritual force streams forth from him and flows through our being also. This fact can neither be shaken nor confirmed by any historical discovery. It is the solid foundation of Christianity.

—*Albert Schweitzer, French theologian, philosopher, and music scholar* (1875–1965)

One drop of Christ's blood is worth more than heaven and earth.

—*Martin Luther* (1483–1546)

I wish he would come in my lifetime so that I could take my crown and lay it at his feet.

—*Queen Victoria* (1819–1901)

All hail the power of Jesus' name!
     Let angels prostrate fall;
Bring forth the royal diadem,
     To crown Him Lord of all!

—*Edward Perronet, English hymn writer and poet* (1726–1792)

I believe that he belongs not only to Christianity but to the entire world, to all races and people; it matters little under what flag, name, or doctrine they may work, profess a faith, or worship a God inherited from the ancestors.

—*Mahatma Gandhi*

Christ shield me this day:
Christ with me,
Christ before me,
Christ behind me,
Christ in me,
Christ beneath me,
Christ above me,
Christ on my right,
Christ on my left,
Christ when I lie down,
Christ when I arise,
Christ in the heart of every person who thinks of me,
Christ in every eye that sees me,
Christ in the ear that hears me.

—*St. Patrick* (387–493)

Seek Christ, and you will find him, and with him everything else thrown in.

—*C. S. Lewis*

He values not Christ at all who does not value Christ above all.

—*St. Augustine*

Above all the grace and the gifts that Christ gives to His beloved is that of overcoming self.

—*St. Francis of Assisi* (1181–1226)

Lord Jesus Christ, Son of God, have mercy on me, a sinner.

—*The Jesus Prayer, 11th century*

Christ, look down upon us; see the desire of so many hearts! You who are Lord of history and Lord of human hearts, be with us! Jesus Christ, eternal Son of God, be with us!

—*Pope John Paul II*

If, then, you are looking for the way by which you should go, take Christ, because he himself is the way.

—*St. Thomas Aquinas* (1225–1274)

May the Babe of Bethlehem be yours to tend;
May the Boy of Nazareth be yours for friend;
May the Man of Galilee his healing send;
May the Christ of Calvary his courage lend;
May the Risen Lord his presence send;
And his holy angels defend you to the end.

—*"Pilgrim's Prayer," found in Oberammergau, West Germany*

Christ is the Alpha and Omega, the beginning and the end of everything. All times and ages belong to Him. To Him be glory forevermore. May the light of Christ, the light of the faith, continue to shine. . . . May no darkness ever extinguish it!

—*Pope John Paul II*

On the Teachings of Jesus

THEN PETER, FILLED WITH THE HOLY SPIRIT, addressed them, 'Rulers of the people, and elders! If you are questioning us today about an act of kindness to a cripple and asking us how he was healed, you must know, all of you, and the whole people of Israel, that it is by the name of Jesus Christ the Nazarene, whom you crucified, and God raised from the dead, by this name and by no other that this man stands before you cured. This is the stone which you, the builders, rejected but which has become the cornerstone. Only in him is there salvation; for of all the names in the world given to men, this is the only one by which we can be saved.'

—*Acts* 4:8–12

On the Day of the Resurrection the truth of Christ's words was confirmed, the Truth that the Kingdom of God has come to us, the Truth of the whole of His messianic mission.

—*Pope John Paul II*

✤

You cannot have forgotten that all of us, when we were baptized into Christ Jesus, were baptized into his death. So by our baptism into his death we were buried with him, so that as Christ was raised from the dead by the Father's glorious power, we too should begin living a new life. If we have been joined to him by dying a death like his, so we shall be by a resurrection like his; realizing that our former self was crucified with him, so that the self which belonged to sin should be destroyed and we should be freed from the slavery of sin. . . . But we believe that, if we died with Christ, then we shall live with him too. We know that Christ has been raised from the dead and will never die again. Death has no power over him any more. For by dying, he is dead to sin once and for all, and now the life that he lives is life with God. In the same way, you must see yourselves as being dead to sin but alive for God in Christ Jesus.

—*Romans* 6:3–11

The cross is the central symbol of Christianity. Many cathedrals have been built in the shape of the cross. Their towers are crowned with the symbol. Every mass is a reenactment of the sacrificial death of Christ. On can hardly turn in any direction without seeing a cross on a hill, on a church, or as a piece of jewelry. This universal symbol is understood by virtually everyone. Its very sight calls to mind Christ's first-century execution. It is his salvation symbol.

—*Calvin Miller, American clergyman and writer* (b. 1936)

Jesus' teaching is not the product of human learning, of whatever kind. It originates from immediate contact with the Father, from "face-to face" dialogue—from the vision of the one who rests close to the Father's heart. It is the Son's word. Without this inner grounding, his teaching would be pure presumption. That is just what the learned men of Jesus' time judged it to be, and they did so precisely because they could not accept its inner grounding: seeing and knowing face-to-face.

—*Pope Benedict XVI* (b. 1927)

To be a Christian is to believe in the impossible. Jesus was God. Jesus was Human.

—*Madeleine L'Engle* (1918–2007)

As often as we are mown down by you, the more we grow in numbers; the blood of Christians is the seed.

—*Tertullian, ecclesiastical writer and Father of the early Church* (c. 160–c. 225)

We Christians, then, do not possess the mystery through wisdom based on Greek reasoning, but in the power given to us by God, through Jesus Christ. As evidence that this is true, you can see that although we are unlettered, we do believe in God and know through his works that his providence cares for all things. We rely on Christ for the truth of our faith, while you rely on sophistry and clever words.

—*St. Anthony of Egypt* (251–356)

We women were allowed to stand at the Cross. We saw His wounds bleed and His eyes grow dim. As He was dying Jesus put His faith in us, we were to carry His love through the whole world and here we sit and have forgotten Him.

—*St. Elizabeth of Thuringia* (1207–1231)

We have resolved to grant to all Christians as well as all others the liberty to practice the religion they prefer, in order that whatever exists of divinity or celestial power may help and favor us and all who are under our government.

—*Constantine the Great, Edict of Milan,* 313

Jesus' central message is that God loves us with an unconditional love and desires our love, free from all fear, in return.

—*Henri J. M. Nouwen*

The Christian who desires to follow Jesus carrying his cross must bear in mind that the name "Christian" means "learner or imitator of Christ" and that if he wishes to bear that noble title worthily he must above all do as Christ charges us in the Gospel; we must oppose or deny ourselves, take up the cross, and follow him.

—*St. Anthony Mary Claret* (1807–1870)

Peace of heart that is won by refusing to bear the common yoke of human sympathy is a peace unworthy of a Christian. To seek tranquility by stopping our ears to the cries of human pain is to make ourselves not Christian but a kind of degenerate stoic having no relation either to stoicism or Christianity.

—*A. W. Tozer, American clergyman and writer,* (1897–1963)

Christianity taught men that love is worth more than intelligence.

—*Jacques Maritain* (1882–1973)

The real security of Christianity is to be found in its benevolent morality, in its exquisite adaptation to the human heart, in the facility with which its scheme accommodates itself to the capacity of every human intellect, in the consolation which it bears to the house of mourning, in the light with which it brightens the great mystery of the grave.

—*Thomas Babington Macaulay, English writer and politician*
(1800–1859)

Of all the systems of morality, ancient or modern, which have come under my observation, none appears to me so pure as that of Jesus.

—*Thomas Jefferson* (1743–1826)

He who will introduce into public affairs the principles of primitive Christianity, will revolutionize the world.

—*Benjamin Franklin* (1706–1790)

The whole message of the Gospel is this: Become like Jesus. We have his self-portrait. When we keep that in front of our eyes, we will soon learn what it means to follow Jesus and become like him.

—*Henri J. M. Nouwen*

Christianity, if false, is not important. If Christianity is true, however, it is of infinite importance. What it cannot be is moderately important.

—*C. S. Lewis*

I now most solemnly impress upon you the truth and beauty of the Christian Religion, as it came from Christ Himself, and the impossibility of your going far wrong if you humbly but heartily respect it.

—*Charles Dickens, in a letter to his son who was leaving for Australia*

Every Christian who is a true imitator and follower of the Nazarene can and must call himself a second Christ and show forth most clearly in his life the entire image of Christ. Oh, if only all Christians were to live up to their vocation, this very land of exile would be changed into a paradise.

—*St. Padre Pio* (1887–1968)

None of us has lived up to the teachings of Christ.

—*Eleanor Roosevelt* (1884–1962)

I believe in Christianity as I believe that the sun has risen, not only because I see it but because I see everything in it.

—*C. S. Lewis*

Christianity is completed Judaism, or it is nothing.

—*Benjamin Disraeli* (1804–1881)

Even those who have renounced Christianity and attack it, in their inmost being still follow the Christian ideal, for hitherto neither their subtlety nor the ardour of their hearts has been able to create a higher ideal of man and of virtue than the ideal given by Christ of old.

—*Fyodor Dostoyevsky*

❖

No Christian can be a pessimist, for Christianity is a system of radical optimism.

—*William R. Inge, English prelate* (1860–1954)

❖

How very hard it is to be A Christian!

—*Robert Browning* (1812–1889)

❖

The Christian ought to live in the perspective of eternity.

—*Pope John Paul II*

Some people feel guilty about their anxieties and regard them as a defect of faith [but] they are afflictions, not sins. Like all afflictions, they are, if we can so take them, our share in the passion of Christ.

—*C. S. Lewis*

Every baptized Christian is obliged by his baptismal promises to renounce sin and to give himself completely, without compromise, to Christ, in order that he may fulfill his vocation, save his soul, enter into the mystery of God, and there find himself perfectly "in the light of Christ."

—*Thomas Merton*

Remember that the Christian life is one of action; not of speech and daydreams.

—*St. Vincent Pallotti* (1795–1850)

Feeding the hungry Christ.
Clothing the naked Christ.
Visiting the sick Christ.
Giving shelter to the homeless Christ.
Teaching the ignorant Christ.

We all long for heaven where God is, but we have it in our power to be in heaven with Him right now—to be happy with Him at this very moment. But being happy with Him now means loving like He loves, helping like He helps, giving as He gives, serving as He serves, rescuing as He rescues, being with Him twenty-four hours a day—touching Him in his distressing disguise.

—*Mother Teresa* (1910–1997)

❖

I believe in the example that Jesus set by feeding the hungry and healing the sick and always prioritizing the least of these over the powerful.

—*Barack Obama* (b. 1961)

Do all the good you can, by all the means you can, in all the ways you can, in all the places you can, at all the times you can, to all the people you can, as long as ever you can.

—*John Wesley, English religious leader* (1703–1791)

Do you want to honor Christ's body? Then do not scorn him in his nakedness, nor honor him here in the church with silken garments while neglecting him outside where he is cold and naked.

—*St. John Chrysostom* (c. 347–407)

My responsibility is always and everywhere the same: to see in my brother more even than the personality and manhood that are his. My task is always and everywhere the same: to see Christ himself.

—*Trevor Huddleston, English clergyman and anti-Apartheid activist* (1913–1998)

The Christian vocation is essentially apostolic. Only in this dimension of service to the Gospel will the Christian find the fullness of his dignity and responsibility.

—*Pope John Paul II*

The true Christian is the true citizen, lofty of purpose, resolute in endeavor, ready for a hero's deeds, but never looking down on his task because it is cast in the day of small things.

—*Theodore Roosevelt* (1858–1919)

A Christian who does not suffer for the sake of Christ and the sake of the kingdom cannot be a Christian. These are the words of Jesus, "Unless you take up your cross and follow me you cannot be my disciple." He says this quite categorically. A church that does not suffer for Christ's sake and the gospel's cannot be the church of Jesus Christ.

—*Desmond M. Tutu* (b. 1931)

If a man cannot be a Christian in the place where he is, he cannot be a Christian anywhere.

—*Henry Ward Beecher* (1813–1887)

The Christian ideal has not been tried and found wanting. It has been found difficult; and left untried.

—*G. K. Chesterton* (1874–1936)

It will be asked, "Who then can be saved, and where shall we find Christians?" . . . Christians are rare people on earth.

—*Martin Luther*

Authentic Christianity never destroys what is good. It makes it grow, transfigures it and enriches itself from it.

—*Claire Huchet Bishop, American writer* (1899–1993)

It is normal and necessary for a mature Christian to have to confront, at some time or other, the inevitable shortcoming of Christians—of others as well as of himself. It is both dishonest and unfaithful for a Christian to imagine that the only way to preserve his faith in the Church is to convince himself that everything is always, in every way, at all times ideal in her life and activity. History is there to prove the contrary. It is unfortunately true that Christians themselves, for one reason or another, may in the name of God himself and of his truth, cling to subtle forms of prejudice, inertia, and mental paralysis. Indeed there may even be serious moral disorders and injustices where holiness should prevail. . . . The Christian must learn how to face these problems with a sincere and humble concern for truth and for the glory of God's Church. He must learn to help correct these errors, without falling into an indiscreet or rebellious zeal. . . .

—*Thomas Merton*

✤

No man can find salvation save in the Catholic Church. Outside the Catholic Church he can find everything save salvation.

—*St. Augustine*

Christians have burnt each other, quite persuaded
That all the Apostles would have done as they did.

—*Lord Byron* (1788–1824)

There is no wild beast so ferocious as Christians who differ
concerning their faith.

—*W. E. H. Lecky, Irish historian* (1838–1903)

Christian religions mix about as well as holy water and holy oil.

—*Barbara Rosewicz, American journalist* (b. 1957)

We should easily convert even the Turks to the obedience of
our gospel, if only we would agree among ourselves and unite
in some holy confederacy.

—*Thomas Cranmer, English clergyman* (1489–1556)

He who begins by loving Christianity better than the truth, will proceed by loving his own sect or Church better than Christianity, and end in loving himself best of all.

—*Samuel Taylor Coleridge* (1772–1834)

Of all the animosities which have existed among mankind, those which are caused by a difference of sentiments in religion appear to be the most inveterate and distressing, and ought most to be deprecated. I was in hopes that the enlightened and liberal policy, which has marked the present age, would at least have reconciled Christians of every denomination so far that we should never again see their religious disputes carried to such a pitch as to endanger the peace of society.

—*George Washington* (1732–1799)

Is it not strange that the descendants of those Pilgrim Fathers who crossed the Atlantic to preserve their own freedom of opinion have always proved themselves intolerant of the spiritual liberty of others?

—*Robert E. Lee* (1807–1870)

In America the taint of sectarianism lies broad upon the land. Not content with acknowledging the supremacy of the Deity, and with erecting temples in his honor, where all can bow down with reverence, the pride and vanity of human reason enter into and pollute our worship, and the houses that should be of God and for God, alone, where he is to be honored with submissive faith, are too often merely schools of metaphysical and useless distinctions. The nation is sectarian, rather than Christian.

—*James Fenimore Cooper* (1789–1851)

✦

I like the silent church before the service begins, better than any preaching.

—*Ralph Waldo Emerson* (1803–1882)

✦

The only way to win audiences is to tell people about the life and death of Christ. Every other approach is a waste.

—*Fulton J. Sheen, American Catholic Bishop and writer* (1895–1979)

Oh priest of Jesus Christ, celebrate this Mass as if it were your first Mass, your only Mass, your last Mass.

—*sign in sacristy of Mother Teresa Hospice, New York City*

The blessings promised us by Christ were not promised to those alone who were priests; woe unto the world, indeed, if all that deserved the name of virtue were shut up in a cloister.

—*Héloise, French abbess* (c.1098–1164)

I want to throw open the windows of the Church so that we can see out and the people can see in.

—*Pope John XXIII* (1881–1963)

The Church's one foundation
Is Jesus Christ, her Lord;
She is His new creation
By water and the Word.

—*Samuel John Stone, American hymn writer* (1839–1901)

The Church is like a great ship being pounded by the waves of life's different stresses. Our duty is not to abandon ship, but to keep her on her course.

—*St. Boniface* (680–754)

Whoever is responsible, the image of the Catholic Church which has been created in the American mind is not an image of the Church of Christ. It is largely an image of a power structure.

—*Norman St. John-Stevas, English politician and writer* (b. 1929)

Anybody can be pope; the proof of this is that I have become one.

—*Pope John XXIII*

Vatican II was a force that seized the mind of the Roman Catholic Church and carried it across centuries from the 13th to the 20th.

—*Lance Morrow, American professor and journalist* (b. 1939)

Christians ought to rise together in defense of spiritual and moral values against the pressure of materialism and moral permissiveness.

—*Pope John Paul II*

There can be neither Jew nor Greek, there can be neither slave nor freeman, there can be neither male nor female—for you are all one in Christ Jesus. And simply by being Christ's, you are that progeny of Abraham, the heirs named in the promise.

—*Galatians,* 3:28–29

Accept one another, then, for the sake of God's glory, as Christ accepted you.

—*Romans* 15:7

All Christians must be committed to dialogue with the believers of all religions, so that mutual understanding and collaboration may grow; so that moral values may be strengthened; so that God may be praised in all creation. Ways must be developed to make this dialogue become a reality everywhere. . . .

—*Pope John Paul II*

❖

I believe in an America where the separation of church and state is absolute—where no Catholic prelate would tell the President (should he be a Catholic) how to act and no Protestant minister would tell his parishioners for whom to vote—where no church or church school is granted any public funds or political preference—and where no man is denied public office merely because his religion differs from the President who might appoint him or the people who might elect him.

—*John F. Kennedy* (1917–1963)

Make sure that no captivates you with the empty lure of a "philosophy" of the kind that human beings hand on, based on the principles of this world and not on Christ.

—*Colossians* 2:8

Christianity, with its doctrine of humility, of forgiveness, of love, is incompatible with the State, with its haughtiness, its violence, its punishment, its wars.

—*Leo Tolstoy*

The church must be reminded that it is not the master or the servant of the state, but rather the conscience of the state.

—*Martin Luther King, Jr.*

The wealthy don't go to church anymore; they go to a museum on Sunday afternoon. That's why we have magnificent museums being built instead of magnificent churches.

—*John Hall Snow, American clergyman and professor* (1924–2008)

If you examined a hundred people who had lost their faith in Christianity, I wonder how many of them would turn out to have reasoned out of it by honest argument? Do not most people simply drift away?

—*C. S. Lewis*

If we were to do the Second Coming of Christ in color for a full hour, there would be a considerable number of stations which would decline to carry it on the grounds that a Western or a quiz show would be more profitable.

—*Edward R. Murrow (1908–1965)*

Who does not see that the same authority which can establish Christianity, in exclusion of all other religions, may establish with the same ease any particular sect of Christians, in exclusion of all other sects?

—*James Madison (1751–1836)*

Do not let Sunday be taken from you . . . If your soul has no Sunday, it becomes an orphan.

—*Albert Schweitzer, French theologian, philosopher, and music scholar* (1875–1965)

We grow in Christ and Christ grows in us. In us, self must die, that we may rise from the grave of what we are, to the glory of what we should be.

—*Sisters of the Holy Nativity, Religious Order of Episcopal Church*

I doubt if there is in the world a single problem, whether social, political, or economic, which would not find read solution if men and nations would rule their lives according to the plain teaching of the Sermon on the Mount.

—*Franklin D. Roosevelt* (1882–1945)

Most people are willing to take the Sermon on the Mount as a flag to sail under, but few will use it as a rudder by which to steer.

—*Oliver Wendell Holmes, American jurist* (1841–1935)

It is time that Christians were judged more by their likeness to Christ than their notions of Christ.

—*Lucretia Mott, American social reformer* (1793–1880)

We ought to love what Christ loved on earth, and to set no store by those things which he regarded as of no account.

—*St. John Vianney* (1786–1859)

If you're going to care about the fall of the sparrow you can't pick and choose who's going to be the sparrow. It's everybody.

—*Madeleine L'Engle*

I don't preach a social gospel; I preach the Gospel, period.
The gospel of our Lord Jesus Christ is concerned for the whole
person. When people were hungry, Jesus didn't say, "Now
is that political, or social?" He said, "I feed you." Because the
good news to a hungry person is bread. . . . If people wish to
say, "God's writ does not run in the political sphere," I want to
ask, "Whose does?"

—*Desmond M. Tutu*

❖

Christianity can never be reduced to a set of rules and
regulations; it is above all a person, Jesus Christ, perfect
God and perfect man. It was he who told the Prince of the
Apostles, "You are Peter, and upon this rock, I will build my
Church, and the gates of hell will not prevail against it." Those
are the tremendous claims of Catholicism: that God became
man and that he founded his Church on the shoulders of a
poor fisherman.

—*Pope John Paul II*

We are learning from the teaching and example of Jesus that life itself is a religion, that nothing is more sacred than a human being, that the end of all right institutions, whether the home or the church or an educational establishment, or a government, is the development of the human soul.

—*Anna Howard Shaw, American physician, minister, and leader in women's rights movement* (1847–1919)

Christianity is not a theory or speculation, but a life; not a philosophy of life, but a life and a living process.

—*Samuel Taylor Coleridge*

Christianity simply does not make sense until you have faced the sort of facts I have been describing. Christianity tells people to repent and promises them forgiveness. It therefore has nothing (as far as I know) to say to people who do not know they have done anything to repent of and who do not feel that they need forgiveness.

—*C. S. Lewis*

The Christian call . . . does not mean we are to become rigid and aggressive moralists with a strict and firm answer to every ethical problem. But it does mean we are committed to the conviction that there is an answer to be found.

—*David H. C. Read, American clergyman, scholar, and writer* (1910–2001)

The religion of Christ is not aspirin to deaden the pain of living, it is not a discussion group, nor a miraculous medal nor a piety, nor bingo for God. Not anything less than a joyous adventure of being Christ in a world still skeptical of him.

—*John Monaghan, American priest, quoted in* New York Journal-American, *February 16, 1961*

This holy exercise of prayer . . . is more essential for a Christian who wants to live a Christian life than are the earth which supports us, the air which we breathe, the bread which sustains us and the heart which beats in our breast necessary to us for human life.

—*St. John Eudes* (1601–1680)

Be good, keep your feet dry, your eyes open, your heart at peace and your soul in the joy of Christ.

—*Thomas Merton*

Christian perfection consists in three things: praying heroically, working heroically, and suffering heroically.

—*St. Anthony Mary Claret* (1807–1870)

Christianity is a rescue religion. It declares that God has taken the initiative in Jesus Christ to deliver us from our sins. This is the main theme of the Bible.

—*John R. W. Stott, English clergyman* (b. 1921)

In all your deeds and words you should look upon this Jesus as your model. Do so whether you are walking or keeping silence, or speaking, whether you are alone or with others. He is perfect, and thus you will be not only irreprehensible, but praiseworthy.

—*St. Bonaventure* (1221–1274)

Jesus' teachings are truly learned only when you become
the teaching. There is already something deeply instinctive
about love in all of us. Yet innate as love may seem, we didn't
become love. We pick and choose whom to give our love
to, but when the switch is turned off, we can be completely
unloving. The lesson about divine love that Jesus taught is that
love is so full of grace, it leads to transformation: it changes a
person's whole being.

—*Deepak Chopra* (b. 1946)

The Christian is in the world but not of the world. . . . His
conduct, his habits of life, his way of thinking, of making
choices, of evaluating things and situations . . . happen in the
light of Christ's words, which are a message of everlasting life.

—*Pope John Paul II*

About the Gospels

MATTHEW

THE FIRST GOSPEL OF THE NEW TESTAMENT is the Gospel of Matthew. It contains twenty-eight chapters.

The Gospel of Matthew was traditionally thought to be the first Gospel written, thus its placement at the beginning of the New Testament. A majority of scholars today, however, reject this opinion in favor of the belief that Mark was most likely the first of the Gospels to be written down. This is supported by the fact, discovered in the nineteenth century, that both Matthew and Luke cite and refer to Mark in their Gospels, but Mark does not refer to either of their Gospels in his work.

Ancient tradition indicated that the author was the apostle and disciple of Jesus named Matthew, but this belief has been abandoned by a majority of modern scholars, in part because Matthew's gospel relies so heavily on the Gospel of Mark and also because if Matthew was indeed the author of the gospel named for him, it is unlikely that he would need any sources besides his own firsthand memories of the time he spent with Jesus.

Modern scholarship attributes the Gospel of Matthew's authorship to an unknown Jewish Christian (still referred to as Matthew for convenience sake) writing for a primarily Jewish Christian audience, possibly in the area of Antioch— the capital of the Roman province of Syria—at least a decade after Mark's Gospel was written. Supporting the theory of the Jewish Christian audience are Matthew's many references to the Old Testament in the Gospel, which presupposes the audience's familiarity with that material.

Matthew's Gospel presents Jesus as the promised Savior of the Old Testament, but one sent to save the entire world rather than just the Jewish people. The Gospel is written meticulously, and includes a description of Jesus' genealogy and his miraculous birth, his baptism and temptations, and then focuses on his teaching, preaching, and healing, and culminates with Jesus' crucifixion and resurrection. The Gospel shows Jesus as a compassionate teacher, who has come to teach the people about the Kingdom of God and the Kingdom of Heaven.

MARK

THE GOSPEL OF MARK IS THE SECOND GOSPEL of the New Testament. It is placed after Matthew and before Luke. It contains sixteen chapters and is the shortest of the four Gospels.

It is one of the Synoptic Gospels, meaning that it has the same view as two of the other Gospels (Matthew and Luke).

The Gospel was most likely written in Rome around A.D. 70, at a time of imminent persecution. Studies of the language used throughout the Gospel, and its infrequent use of quotes from the Old Testament, reveal that the intended audience was probably Gentiles, unfamiliar with Jewish tradition.

Though the Gospel is written anonymously, it is attributed to Mark the Evangelist, also known as John Mark, a cousin of Barnabas and companion of St. Paul. Other sources indicate the author may have been a disciple of St. Peter, and the author is sometimes referred to as Peter's translator or interpreter.

The Gospel of Mark has a swift-paced narrative, portraying Jesus as a man of action and authority. The emphasis is placed on Jesus as the Son of God and the Messiah prophesied in the Old Testament. There is no information provided about Jesus prior to his baptism and ministry. In this Gospel, Jesus' divinity is revealed by his actions—such as forgiving sins and casting out demons—rather than through his words or teachings alone.

The earliest manuscripts of Mark's Gospel do not include appearances by the risen Jesus but ends at the empty tomb. The material called the Longer Ending, which includes appearances of the risen Christ, has generally been accepted as a canonical part of the Gospel but is likely to have been written by someone other than Mark.

LUKE

LUKE IS THE THIRD GOSPEL, coming after Mark and before John. Containing twenty-four chapters, it is the longest of the four Gospels.

Another of the Synoptic Gospels, Luke's was written, according to many scholars, in A.D. 80–90 for an audience of Gentile Christians.

Tradition dating back to the late second century indicates the author of the Gospel to be Luke, a Gentile Christian who may have been a companion of St. Paul. Luke is also regarded as the author of the Acts of the Apostles. Some traditions indicate that Luke was a physician, yet there has been little evidence found in the text of the Gospel to corroborate this.

The Gospel begins with a recounting of the Annunciation to Mary that she will be the Mother of God, followed by the birth of John the Baptist, Jesus' birth, and his infancy. Luke's Gospel then follows the same outline as Matthew and Mark. Luke presents Jesus as the Savior as promised in the Old Testament and of all mankind. There is an emphasis on Jesus' caring and mercy to the poor, lowly, and downtrodden, and also a special emphasis on the Holy Spirit, prayer, and the role of women in the Gospel.

JOHN

THE GOSPEL OF JOHN IS THE FOURTH BOOK in the New Testament, coming after Luke and before the Acts of the Apostles. The Gospel contains twenty-one chapters.

John's Gospel was probably written near the end of the first century, perhaps for an audience of Greek-speaking Jews in either Antioch or Ephesus. This Gospel was traditionally thought to have been written by Jesus' apostle John. Some modern scholars, however, think the author was actually a follower or several followers of John the apostle.

The Gospel stands apart from the three Synoptic Gospels in several respects. It doesn't follow the same order or repeat the same stories as the other three Gospels and begins with a stirring prologue that presents Jesus as the eternal Word of God, stating many of the themes contained in the Gospel.

John's Gospel presents various miracles or "signs" which support Jesus as the Savior and Son of God and proceeds to explain what the miracles reveal. The next chapters record the night of Jesus' arrest and the fellowship he shared with his disciples on the night before his crucifixion. The Gospel's final chapters detail Jesus' arrest, trial, crucifixion, resurrection, and his appearances to his disciples after his resurrection.

In its conclusion, the Gospel states that it was written so that readers might believe that Jesus is the promised Savior, the Son of God, and that through their faith in him they might have life. (20:31).

Throughout the Gospel there are instances of striking symbolism where ordinary items— such as water, bread, light, the shepherd and his sheep, and grapes and the grapevine—are used to reveal spiritual truths.